Why Does Grandma Have a Wibble?

Heidi Krumenauer

WinePress Publishing (PO Box 428, Enumclaw, WA 98022) functions only as book publisher. As such, the ultimate design, content, editorial accuracy, and views expressed or implied in this work are those of the author.

ISBN 13: 978-1-57921-913-0
ISBN 10: 1-57921-913-6
Library of Congress Catalog Card Number: 2007927288

Printed in Korea.

Dedication

To my grandmothers – Clara and Doris.
Thanks for all your cookies, for playing games and for hugs whenever I needed them.
You're treasured gifts.
I love you and miss you both so much.

To my mom, JoAnn – who is the definition of a magnificent grandparent.
Thank you for the love you shower upon my sons. I can only hope to do it as well as you someday.
I love you.

Acknowledgements

To my dear son Noah:

Your adoration of and wonder about Grandma's "wibble" has been the inspiration for so many other children to voice their love and curiosity of their own grandmothers. Thank you! I love you so much!

To Mom:

Thanks for letting Noah adore your "wibble"! And thank you, too, for all your coordination of this project. I couldn't have made it without you.

To Jeff:

You've read all these quotes and so many more, and you've played "assistant" on so many occasions! Thank you for all the love and support you continue to give to my writing projects. And thanks for "enjoying the ride" with me. I love you!

To Payton:

Thank you for sitting next to me while I worked on this project. That made all the hours on the computer much more bearable. I love you!

Special thanks to the children and teachers in the Monroe School District. Without you, this book wouldn't exist!

Grandmas hold our tiny hands for just a little while, but our hearts forever.

~Author Unknown

Contents

What do you want to ask your grandma?

What do you want to ask your grandma?

When is Valentine's Day in Florida?

~McKenzie, 9

Why do you collect checks and mail?

~Samantha, 8

Who was your first boyfriend and what did you do on your first date?

~Holly, 11

What do you want to ask your grandma?

How did you meet Grandpa?

~Hannah, 8

Why are you so emotional?

~Matea, 8

Did you have a pet when you were little?

~Chelsea, 10

Why do you have a wibble?

~Noah, 7

Alysha, 7

What do you want to ask your grandma?

Can I come to your house? I miss you so much.

~Payton, 5

How old are you?

~Caleb, 12

Do you have real teeth?

~Sabrina, 9

What do you want to ask your grandma?

What makes you laugh?

~Trent, 4

How were you born?

~Kerstin, 5

If I was a bubble, could I fly up to Heaven and bring you back?

~Victor, 5

Why do you have a bow and arrow?

What do you want to ask your grandma?

Why do you give the dog the first pancake?

~Dontae`, 9

What are you doing when I'm not there?

~Kristy, 8

What is your middle name?

~Hunter, 7

Why do you snore?

~Nick, 5

What do you want to ask your grandma?

Who are your grandparents?

~Martina, 12

Are you scared of the dark?

~Ti, 8

Do you like having a lot of kids?

~Ally, 8

Brittany, 7

What do you want to ask your grandma?

How often do you see my dad? Does he ever ask about me?

–Julie, 11

Why do you go to Mexico every year when it's cold?

–Brady, 5

What's your last name?

–Trenten, 7

What do you want to ask your grandma?

Why is your bed kind of big?

~Nathan, 6

Do you ever wonder what Grandpa is doing in heaven?

~Kelsea, 9

Will I have a wibble when I grow up?

~Katrina, 10

Do you have strong muscles?

What do you want to ask your grandma?

What did you do when you were my age?

~Rachel, 11

Why do you like tomatoes?

~Hayley, 11

When is your birthday? I always forget!

~Ellis, 8

Were there cars back in your day?

~Alyssa, 10

What do you want to ask your grandma?

Why did you marry Grandpa?

~Dana, 11

Would you jump off a cliff for a billion dollars?

~Kirsten, 10

Why do we come over to your house on holidays?

~Grace, 6

Catie, 5

What do you want to ask your grandma?

What did your parents do for a living?

~Max, 10

Why do you take lots of pills?

~Braden, 7

Why do you have blue eyes?

~Keagen, 7

What do you want to ask your grandma?

Do you have any black hair at all or is it all gray?

~Sabrina, 9

How do you have time to make desserts every day?

~Mariah, 11

Could I live with you?

~Jessica, 12

Dakota, 6

What do you want to ask your grandma?

How old are you going to live to be?

~Mikhaila, 13

What were your "ansisters" like?

~Autumn, 12

How do you clean so beautifully?

~Emma, 7

What do you want to ask your grandma?

What did you want to be when you grew up?

~Samantha, 11

Why do you just sit on the couch and go to church?

~Maddy, 7

Are you related to an Egyptian?

~Lauren, 10

Emma, 7

What do you want to ask your grandma?

How do you grow a garden so fast?

~Brittany, 7

Did you go to college?

~Mitch, 12

Do you have your own teeth or not?

~Alyssa, 5

How did you get cancer?

~Ben, 11

What do you want to ask your grandma?

Why do you do so much man work?

~Cody, 9

Could you get me a pair of teeth like yours?

~Ashley, 12

Could you make more cookies? They are so good!

~Brooke, 8

Marquel, 8

What do you want to ask your grandma?

Who are your parents?

~Payton, 12

Do you take a shower every day?

~Hayden, 5

Who's your favorite grandchild?

~Alicia, 8

Do you like the color red?

~Mariah, 6

What do you want to ask your grandma?

How did you treat Mom and her brothers when they were little?

~Brianna, 11

What was your childhood like?

~Becca, 11

Have you ever dyed your hair blonde?

~Michaela, 11

Makaila, 5

What do you want to ask your grandma?

Would you like to be famous someday?

–Lauren, 11

Are you happy?

–Garrett, 8

Are you lonely 'cuz Papa can't watch TV with you 'cuz he has to sleep through the day 'cuz he has to work at night?

–Xena, 6

What do you want to ask your grandma?

Why are you so old?

~Cole, 6

Do you like to take naps?

~Dakota, 4

How do you make your bread?

~Michelle, 8

Why are you so goofy?

~Devon, 6

Frances, 5

What do you want to ask your grandma?

How old were you when you thought Grandpa was cute?

~Kirsten, 10

Do you have children?

~Stephanie, 7

What was it like when you won the lottery?

~Josh, 12

What do you want to ask your grandma?

What was it like when you found out you were going to be a grandma?

~Karlie, 12

Do you ever get tired of picking berries and making them into jelly?

~Tanner, 9

Did you get any valentines?

~Dana, 6

Hannah, 4

What do you want to ask your grandma?

Are you my friend?

~Amanda, 6

Why do you always insist on doing everything yourself and not have too much help with it? Like that you push your own wheelchair.

~Oliver, 12

What was your first car?

~Casey, 9

What do you want to ask your grandma?

How do you make that chocolate cake so good?

—Samantha, 8

How much do you love me?

—Alysha, 7

Do you change your socks every day?

—Benjamin, 11

Hayden, 6

What do you want to ask your grandma?

How do you know how to help me?

–Anthany, 5

Would you give up your farm for me?

–Cody, 10

Would you buy me a shirt?

–Jesse, 6

Are you rich now?

–Gabe, 12

What do you want to ask your grandma?

When are you going to get me a birthday present?

~Alisa, 7

How do you get ready for all the people who come over at Christmastime?

~Abby, 11

What is your favorite thing to bake?

~Breawn, 11

Heath, 4

What do you want to ask your grandma?

What did your mom and dad look like?

–Briana, 8

When was your first kiss?

–Anna, 8

How was it growing up without a TV or computer or even video games? I think you must have played outside a lot.

–Paige, 10

What do you want to ask your grandma?

How do you run so fast?

~Irbin, 12

Why do you wear a T-shirt in the winter?

~Kaylee, 5

How do you get beautiful hair?

~Ben, 5

How do you still move around at your age?

~ShiAnne, 11

Jacob, 6

What do you want to ask your grandma?

What was your favorite toy?

~Sommer, 7

Do you have a job?

~Erick, 8

How much money have you made gambling?

~Alex, 12

How are you so good at believing God?

~CJ, 8

What do you want to ask your grandma?

How do you live without Grandpa in your life?

~Emily, 9

What is one of my characteristics that you like best?

~Ashley, 11

Why do you sleep with Grandpa?

~Cindy, 5

Jacob, 7

What do you want to ask your grandma?

Could I have seven dollars?

—Santana, 10

How did you feel when Grandpa went to Vietnam?

—Lane, 11

Why do you make every sentence confusing? Some words you say I don't even think are words.

—Leeza, 12

What do you want to ask your grandma?

How much do you weigh?

~Nate, 7

When were you born?

~Amanda, 7

Why do your arms jiggle on the bottom like that? That scares me.

~Jordin, 11

Jenna, 8

What do you want to ask your grandma?

Were you smart when you were little?

~Kyle, 8

How do you whistle so good?

~Liam, 7

What's your real name?

~Hunter, 8

Can I have Grandpa's truck?

~Trevor, 12

What do you want to ask your grandma?

Did you have a crush when you were a teenager?

~Autumn, 8

What are your favorite colors? I want to make pillows and scarves for you.

~Briana, 11

Where is my rat?

~Mason, 6

Jordan, 8

What do you want to ask your grandma?

How did you learn how to knit?

~Alysha, 7

What's your recipe for your cookies?

~Cody, 8

What was it like back in the olden days?

~Nick, 7

Why do you have lots of houses?

~Ezrie, 5

What do you want to ask your grandma?

Could I have a million dollars?

~Brad, 12

Was my dad as good as he said he was when he was growing up?

~Nathan, 8

Were you alive when Martin Luther King was and did you hear his speech?

~Kailey, 8

Josh, 12

What do you want to ask your grandma?

How many boyfriends did you have in your whole lifetime?

~Irby, 12

Will you fix my Spiderman costume?

~Jacob, 5

How much money did you make at your first job?

~Elizabeth, 12

What do you want to ask your grandma?

How do you clean up the messes we make?

~Mikhaila, 13

How do you carry heavy stuff?

~Derek, 6

How are you doing?

~Jarrett, 7

Why does your voice sound so young?

~Noah, 8

Kara, 6

What do you want to ask your grandma?

What did you look like when you were little?

~Elizabeth, 8

What's your middle name?

~Jason, 12

Did you love your wedding dress?

~Dana, 10

What do you want to ask your grandma?

What was her childhood like? She never really got to tell me before she died.

~Brandy, 11

How old were you when you married Grandpa?

~Brianna, 11

Why do you always go to the zoo when it's not even time?

~Nick, 6

Kyle, 8

What do you want to ask your grandma?

Can you get a trampoline in your yard?

~Andrew, 8

What was my granddad like?

~Hannah, 11

How did you get all your cool stuff?

~Jenna, 8

Were you naughty when you were little?

~Parker, 8

What do you want to ask your grandma?

Do you think you look young?

~Jared, 11

What's your first name?

~Grace, 6

If you could have any wish, what would it be?

~Ally, 8

I know everything about Granny!

~Olivia, 7

Mason, 6

What is the most interesting thing about your grandma?

What is the most interesting thing about your grandma?

She has style.

~Taren, 8

She's still alive.

~Brittany, 9

Not much.

~Kyler, 8

She takes care of me and she loves me.

~Morgan, 8

What is the most interesting thing about your grandma?

She paints her toenails red.

~Lisa, 8

She is always cleaning the house.

~Aaron, 12

She's best at loving.

~Cade, 7

She actually goes out of town.

~Ethan, 9

Megan, 8

What is the most interesting thing about your grandma?

She is old, but she can still find the time and energy to go out and do things.

~Oliver, 12

She drives a semitruck.

~Samantha, 11

She is happy all the time.

~Alex, 8

What is the most interesting thing about your grandma?

She lives on a farm.

~Wyatt, 6

She gave me these trees and said they wouldn't die, but they did.

~Tiva, 7

She has a big house with a lot of stuff to mess around with.

~Jared, 12

She has really curly hair.

What is the most interesting thing about your grandma?

She knows her grandkids' every move.

~Dominique, 12

She's a major part of her community.

~Alexis, 12

She loves to spoil me.

~Whitney, 7

She's not a slow driver!

~Alyssa, 10

What is the most interesting thing about your grandma?

She's in her 80's and she is still alive, and that's a good thing!

~Tabitha, 11

She smells bad when she comes in from the barn.

~Cole, 7

She can ride a unicycle.

~Dontae`, 9

She dances a lot.

What is the most interesting thing about your grandma?

She looks so young.

~Nick, 7

She is very, very, very religious.

~A.J., 11

She doesn't have any video games for herself.

~Zackary, 5

What is the most interesting thing about your grandma?

She's an awesome cook.

–Cameron, 8

She gets up early and milks cows.

–Haley, 6

She lives with me.

–Tala, 7

Megan, 8

What is the most interesting thing about your grandma?

Most grandmas have white hair but my grandma doesn't.

~Jack, 7

She's really old, but she doesn't have a wibble.

~Tony, 10

She never, ever says no.

~Amber, 10

What is the most interesting thing about your grandma?

She paints on saws.

~Kaylea, 12

She can't walk, but she can go super fast in her wheelchair.

~Nick, 8

She's a writer and she has written several books and has been published in many magazines.

~Jocelyn, 12

Meghan, 8

What is the most interesting thing about your grandma?

She can paint a picture in four minutes.

~Jarod, 9

She helps other people.

~Chase, 7

Her face looks nice.

~Shekinah, 6

She always wears dress shoes.

~Sierra, 8

What is the most interesting thing about your grandma?

She doesn't like thin mints!

~Lucas, 9

She still has a really good imagination.

~Nickolas, 10

She knits so fast and when she's done, there's no holes!

~Maija, 8

Morgan, 8

What is the most interesting thing about your grandma?

She can talk in Polish and German.

~CJ, 8

When she gets frustrated, she doesn't say bad words.

~Kaya, 8

She collects hats and bullhorns.

~Amanda, 7

What is the most interesting thing about your grandma?

When she was little, she was traveling in a covered wagon, and it broke so they stayed in Illinois.

~Anna, 8

She has good ideas and the friendliest heart.

~April, 9

She likes rap music.

~Kody, 9

Meghan, 9

What is the most interesting thing about your grandma?

She's really, really old, but she's really healthy and in good shape.

~Sadie, 11

She's really good at playing the piano.

~Anika, 12

She loves me the mostest.

~Jamison, 5

What is the most interesting thing about your grandma?

She has been to different places in the world.

–Kieran, 6

She owned a cheese factory and raised five kids at the same time.

–Mitch, 11

She saw her first movie in 4th grade.

–Kaitlyn, 9

Michael, 8

What is the most interesting thing about your grandma?

She can take her teeth out.

–Alysha, 7

She has the same birthday as me.

–Briana, 11

She knows a lot about history.

–Kieran, 6

What is the most interesting thing about your grandma?

She can teach her grandchildren things.

~Isaac, 8

She takes so long to look good in the morning.

~Becca, 11

She is always doing something. She's never laying around doing nothing.

~Catherine, 6

What is the most interesting thing about your grandma?

She always has something purple with her.

~Abby, 8

Her handwriting isn't shaky.

~Katie, 9

She is a pretty woman.

~Sommer, 7

What is the funniest thing you know about your grandma?

What is the funniest thing you know about your grandma?

Nothing.

~Konner, 9

She snored so loud, it woke me up.

~Tessa, 11

She can toot – really, really quiet.

~Andrew, 3

What is the funniest thing you know about your grandma?

She misplaced something and called us to help her find it and it was on her table the whole time.

~Noah, 11

She drove me to school when I was not even in the car!

~Kody, 10

She ate my lunch all gone!

~Jamison, 5

Olivia, 7

What is the funniest thing you know about your grandma?

In France, she tripped so she said: "Oaf!" All the French people started laughing at her because *oaf* means egg in French.

–Ellis, 8

She forgot to wear her skirt to work.

–Shannon, 9

She can't make cakes.

–Robert, 5

What is the funniest thing you know about your grandma?

She scared Grandpa.

~Chase, 7

She picked up a stray cat and brought it inside the house even though Grandpa is allergic to cats.

~Alex, 11

She bought a computer but she does not seem like that kind of person.

~Oliver, 12

Olivia, 7

What is the funniest thing you know about your grandma?

She farted and then said there was an elephant under the table.

—Jessica, 12

She snuck my food when I wasn't looking.

—Jonathan, 8

She tried dancing to my kind of music and it got too fast for her.

—Karlie, 12

What is the funniest thing you know about your grandma?

She went into a store with dog poop on her shoe.

~Shawna, 11

She tasted my sand cake and thought it was real.

~Meghan, 8

Nickolas, 6

What is the funniest thing you know about your grandma?

She was getting something out of the refrigerator and she accidentally let the cat in.

~Brittney, 9

She snorts when she laughs.

~Briana, 8

She made my dad wear pink.

~Kieran, 6

What is the funniest thing you know about your grandma?

She called me Maddie and that's my dog's name.

~Maija, 8

A seagull plopped poop on her head when we were at the beach.

~Alex, 10

Nothing . . . she just had back surgery.

~Maddy, 7

Payton, 5

What is the funniest thing you know about your grandma?

She rakes a lot and she never seems tired.

~Chloe, 8

She taught her dog to how to lay on his back and say his prayers.

~Vincent, 11

She picked up a dead mouse and scared Grandpa with it.

~Trinity, 6

What is the funniest thing you know about your grandma?

She went to [the casino] and came home at 3 a.m.

~Tristin, 9

She gets up every night and gets a drink of water.

~Mariahna, 10

She gave me little spoons.

~Jesse, 6

What is the funniest thing you know about your grandma?

She coughed and sneezed at the same time.

~Mark, 10

It takes both grandmas about 45 minutes to get ready to go somewhere!

~Sky, 9

What is the funniest thing you know about your grandma?

When a man came in the night to her house, she picked up the fireplace poker and beat him with it until he ran out of the house.

–Danielle, 11

She made a sandwich and put the jelly on before the peanut butter.

–Trenten, 7

What is the funniest thing you know about your grandma?

She fell asleep when someone was talking to her.

~Morgan, 8

She went too fast for me in her wheelchair in the nursing home.

~Nick, 8

I think it's funny when Grandma . . .

. . . thinks I'm funny too.

~Brittany, 7

. . . kicks the dog.

~Josi, 7

. . . is talking to someone and in the middle of her sentence she forgets what they're talking about.

~Holly, 11

I think it's funny when Grandma . . .

. . . tries to understand what the singers are saying when she listens to rap and rock music.

~Alec, 12

. . . tells me a funny joke.

~Jacob, 7

. . . picks on Grandpa.

~Ben, 12

Sami, 6

I think it's funny when Grandma . . .

. . . acts younger than her age.

~Courtney, 12

. . . gets me mixed up with my sister.

~Hannah, 8

. . . rolls her eyes back in her head and makes me laugh.

~Mataya, 6

I think it's funny when Grandma . . .

. . . does the Noodle-Poodle Dance when she walks down the street.

~Megan, 9

. . . does Elvis impressions.

~Ryan, 10

. . . laughs when something isn't funny.

~Morgan, 6

Shane, 6

I think it's funny when Grandma . . .

. . . makes a mistake.

–Hassan, 7

. . . dances with my toy lion.

–Anthany, 5

. . . talks about boys.

–Jessica, 12

I think it's funny when Grandma . . .

. . . tries to make jokes.

~Chloe, 8

. . . dresses up like Mrs. Claus at Christmas.

~Cori, 10

. . . pops out her eyes and plays peek-a-boo.

~Bradley, 6

ShiAnne, 11

I think it's funny when Grandma . . .

. . . shivers for no reason.

~Holden, 8

. . . forgets to close the refrigerator when she is in a hurry.

~Dominique, 12

. . . talks without her dentures.

~Chris, 8

I think it's funny when Grandma . . .

. . . rides a four-wheeler and goes so slow.

~Aaron, 11

. . . says "Stop getting so big!"

~Carter, 5

. . . puts the wrong things in the cookies and they don't taste right!

~Michaela, 8

Silas, 8

I think it's funny when Grandma . . .

. . . thinks she made a joke but she didn't.

~Graysen, 11

. . . yells at Grandpa.

~Nick, 8

. . . says I'm an Old Whippersnapper!

~Alexander, 9

. . . left my dog and he was mad.

~Dana, 6

I think it's funny when Grandma . . .

. . . gets mad when her picture is taken.

~Morgan, 10

. . . toots sometimes.

~Madison, 6

. . . plays games she's never played before. She gets the rules mixed up and still ends up winning.

~Kristine, 12

Taylor, 5

I think it's funny when Grandma . . .

. . . uses her hands when she eats.

~Brett, 7

. . . plays jumping jacks.

~Drew, 4

. . . farts and burps and blames it on the bunny rabbits.

~Dana, 10

I think it's funny when Grandma . . .

. . . does her breathing exercises in the car because my grandpa is driving too fast. She takes deep breaths and gets a scared look on her face.

~Caitlyn, 12

. . . screams because there is a bat the living room.

~Thomas, 8

. . . repeats herself.

~Lane, 11

I Love you too
I Love you Grandma
Taylor, 7

I think it's funny when Grandma . . .

. . . looks over her glasses at me.

~Matea, 5

. . . used to tickle my nose. I liked it!

~Cole, 6

. . . always oversleeps like an orangutan.

~Nick, 6

I think it's funny when Grandma . . .

. . . plays her games on the computer because she doesn't know how to use the mouse.

~Tiva, 7

. . . watches James Bond movies.

~Jesse, 9

. . . says "fetch me that because you still got more energy."

~Jessica, 12

Trevor, 6

I think it's funny when Grandma . . .

. . . says "get out of the way" in the Wal-Mart parking lot.

~Michaela, 11

. . . looks for her glasses when they're on top of her head!

~Cayla, 6

. . . squirts water out of her eye.

~Hunter, 6

I think it's funny when Grandma . . .

. . . laughs – because her whole body shakes.

–Lisa, 8

. . . was blind and she would guess who the people were.

–Danielle, 11

What do you love most about your grandma?

What do you love most about your grandma?

I just love her cheeks and her neck. They are soft and they move.

~Matea, 5

She gives us money if we get good grades.

~Isabel, 8

Her personality is just like mine.

~Kari, 9

What do you love most about your grandma?

She worries about me and my brother and sisters.

~Breawn, 11

She listens to my problems and helps me solve them.

~Eliah, 8

I love being her best friend.

~Jamison, 5

What do you love most about your grandma?

Sometimes we plant flowers.

~Dakota, 6

She doesn't make me do a lot of chores.

~Leeza, 12

She's funny.

~Hannah, 12

She cares about anyone or anything.

~Veronica, 12

What do you love most about your grandma?

She tucks me into bed.

~Grant, 5

I love it when she makes pie.

~Sarah, 7

Her hair.

~Suzi, 6

Her carrot cake.

~Kyle, 6

Treyvor, 7

What do you love most about your grandma?

Her smile.

~Kasey, 12

Her baking.

~Dillion, 7

Her generosity.

~Paige, 9

She bakes cookies with me.

~Olivia, 7

What do you love most about your grandma?

I love her squooshy belly.

~Logan, 5

She hugs me. It's warm.

~Ross, 8

She lets me milk the cows.

~Keagen, 7

I love her purse.

~Kaiden, 4

What do you love most about your grandma?

She plays games with me.

~Joe, 7

She is nice and calm about everything.

~Jorlyn, 11

She loves to hear what we have done.

~Monica, 10

I love that she is my mom's mom.

~Tori, 8

What do you love most about your grandma?

She plays dragon and castle with me.

~Charrley, 5

She is never mean.

~Baylie, 8

We go to places and discover things like rocks and plants and wood.

~Amara, 9

Tyler, 8

What do you love most about your grandma?

She loves spending time with me.

~Chelsea, 10

She lets me sleep over.

~Taryn, 6

She knows a lot about everything.

~Mitch, 9

She never gets mad.

~Joe, 12

What do you love most about your grandma?

She helps me out on emotional things like helping me to be a better person.

~Alexis, 12

She tickles me.

~Raven, 7

She loves me back!

~Caroline, 7

What do you love most about your grandma?

She's always joking around.

~Ben, 11

She lets me stay up late.

~Alexander, 9

She understands me.

~Alex, 12

She is old, but she acts like me now.

~Emily, 9

What do you love most about your grandma?

I love it when she holds my hand.

–Alyssa, 9

She always has time.

–Autumn, 12

She rubs my feet at night and it relaxes me and I fall asleep.

–Abby, 8

Veronica, 4

What do you love most about your grandma?

She calls me every day so I can talk to her.

~Noah, 11

When my parents tell me I can't have one of Grandma's wonderful cookies, she sneaks one to me anyway and gives me a wink.

~Anika, 12

She gives me the biggest piece of pie.

~Jacob, 7

What do you love most about your grandma?

She lets me make forts out of her furniture.

~Matt, 5

She takes care of me.

~Ethan, 12

She sews and makes quilts for me and my family.

~Heather, 12

What do you love most about your grandma?

She is loving, caring and respectful to everyone and everything.

~Shawna, 11

She takes me places.

~Sommer, 7

She is nice, cheerful, and careful.

~Mitchell, 8

What do you love most about your grandma?

We rock in her rocking chair.

~Raven, 7

I love it when she makes my birthday cake.

~Jacy, 8

She's serious yet fun.

~Michael, 12

She lets me have midnight snacks.

~Vicki, 9

Whitney, 7

What do you love most about your grandma?

She lives close to us and I don't have to travel that far to see her.

~Hannah, 9

She loves me no matter what happens to me.

~Macayla, 11

She sticks up for me.

~Tessa, 11

What do you love most about your grandma?

She takes time to play with me.

~Anna, 10

If I am sad, she can always make me happy.

~Abby, 11

She fights to stay alive.

~Mark, 10

What do you love most about your grandma?

She's always there when I need her.

~Briana, 11

I love when she reads books to me.

~Trevor, 6

She's always nice to me.

~Nick, 8

She spoils me.

~Cassie, 7

What do you love most about your grandma?

She brings me to the park.

~Abbie, 5

She never really yells.

~Jason, 12

She makes cookies.

~Hassan, 7

She lets me get messy.

~Meghan, 8

Zach, 7

What do you love most about your grandma?

She lets me eat a lot of pickles and olives.

~Zoe, 6

She has a good sense of humor.

~Ben, 8

She has the same name as me.

~Shelby, 11

She doesn't let me get spoiled.

~Tristain, 10

What do you love most about your grandma?

She makes good toast and pancakes and eggs.

~Josh, 10

She laughs at my jokes.

~Nick, 5

She gets me into conversations. She always includes me.

~Sierra, 11

What do you love most about your grandma?

I love the way she teaches me how to do things.

~Jessica, 12

She buys me presents even when it's not my birthday or Christmas.

~Shawn, 10

She doesn't swear.

~ShiAnne, 11

What do you love most about your grandma?

She is the best in the world!

~Jonathan, 9

She's interested in the things I am.

~Jared, 11

She's not like most grandmas - she's unique.

~Jocelyn, 12

Head, Shoulders...Wibble?
Head, Shoulder, Knees, and wibble, Knees and Wibble!!
?
Uh, Grandma?
Home Sweet Home

Alex, 11